THE YALE SERIES OF YOUNGER POETS

45

EDITED BY W. H. AUDEN

POEMS BY JOAN MURRAY

PUBLISHED

ON THE MARY CADY TEW

MEMORIAL FUND

POEMS

BY JOAN MURRAY

1917–1942

EDITED BY GRANT CODE

WITH A FOREWORD BY

W. H. AUDEN

NEW HAVEN

YALE UNIVERSITY PRESS

LONDON · GEOFFREY CUMBERLEGE · OXFORD UNIVERSITY PRESS

1947

Thanks are due to the editors of *Decision* for permission to reprint "Orpheus" and to *Chimera* for permission to reprint "Even the Gulls of the Cool Atlantic."

FOREWORD

I SHOULD like to think that the day will come when the mere fact that a poet is published in The Yale Series of Younger Poets will be recommendation enough. I am somewhat doubtful about the present practice of having a new poet introduced to the public by an older one because my personal reaction as a reader to an announcement of a volume of poems with a foreword by somebody else is a suspicion that the publishers are afraid that the poems are not very good and want reassurance.

Nor do I care much for that so frequently used adjective "promising." If by "promising" one means, "These poems are no good in themselves but lead me to believe that you will write good ones in time," then the poems should not be published, and their author should be expected to wait till he has justified the critics' belief by producing some good poems. One should never publish work of which one thinks poorly just to encourage the author; genuine talent is tougher than that. If, on the other hand, by "promising" one means, "These poems are good and lead me to believe that you will continue to develop and write more good poems, probably quite different from these," that is something which can be said of every real poet at any stage in his career; if his work ceases to be promising in this sense, he has ceased to be a poet.

In the present instance, I should like to emphasize this point because Miss Joan Murray died at the age of twenty-four. We are not publishing her poems out of charity, because she will never be able to write any more, but because they are good, and I hope that the reader will approach her work just as objectively as if she were still alive, and not be distracted by sentimental speculation about what she might have written in the future which was denied her.

Nearly every good poet has certain emotions and imagery which

5

recur and predominate in the work; that is what makes parody possible, and bad poetry, it should be remarked, cannot be parodied because there is no original vision and manner to exaggerate. So, in Miss Murray's poetry, the dominant emotion is, I think, a feeling of isolation, and her characteristic images tactile shapes which reassure her that "Here" and "There" are both real and related to each other. In her own words: "We were lovers of things beyond our bodies."

But a critical discussion of poetry presupposes that the reader is already well familiar with the text, and is therefore out of place, I think, in the case of a new poet who has still to be read. I shall merely suggest to anyone who picks up this volume in a bookstore to open it and read, say, "You Talk of Art," "An Epithalamium," "Even the Gulls of the Cool Atlantic," and "Orpheus." I am confident that, if he is a true judge and lover of poetry, he will neither leave the store without taking the volume with him, nor ever regret his purchase.

W. H. AUDEN

EDITOR'S NOTE

WHEN Joan Murray's manuscripts were placed in my hands for editing, they were in confusion, pages of prose mixed with pages of verse and scarcely two pages of anything together that belonged together. The first task was to separate prose from verse and to sort and arrange the verse, bringing the several pages of each long poem together and the several drafts of poems of which there was more than one copy.

A reading then showed that the poet had not prepared a final text of most of her poems. Many existed in several different versions. Many carried manuscript corrections. They had not been carefully punctuated and the poet's spelling was capricious, occasionally making it difficult to determine what word was meant. It was therefore necessary to make a variorum text of each poem, transferring to one copy all variants, and at the same time solving problems of spelling and correcting spelling when there was no real problem.

A text had then to be established by careful consideration of the variant readings. Where it seemed that the poet had arrived at a final version, this was respected, though occasionally an earlier reading was preferred or something cut was restored. Where the poet did not seem to have established a final reading, what seemed to be the best of her several readings was used, with due consideration of her general feelings, thoughts, and practice in style.

It was then necessary to punctuate in such a way as to make the meaning and syntax clear. The poet's style is highly colloquial and often conversational, not primarily literary, and this is the most difficult sort of style to punctuate. I am fairly confident that the punctuation adopted represents the intention of the poet's meaning.

Finally it was necessary to make a few corrections, such as changing the form of a word for the sake of syntax, or inserting a color-less connective that had been omitted.

I have usually been able to avoid changing any significant word even though the choice of word was highly questionable, such as the use of one part of speech for another or the use of a word in a questionable sense. It is evident that some words had for the poet a peculiar flavor apart from their meaning or their ordinary con-notations and that she used them for this flavor. These peculiarities are of the essence of the poet's style. I am opposed to the practice of trying to "improve" the work of poets, as was done with the poems of Emily Dickinson. The important thing is to preserve exactly what the poet wrote. Any reader is at liberty to have his own opinion about what the poet meant to say. In some lines it seems to me that the poet has been unable to think of the exact word she wished to use and has written in some word as a makeshift to fill out the line, intended to find the exact word later and make a correction. This practice is indeed proved by some of the manuscript corrections. With one exception, I have left these words as she wrote them. Since they are usually related by connotation with the desired sense, they have a curious power of suggestion. In one line I sub-stituted the word "convivial" for "connubial," which was obviously not the right word and had a disturbing effect. In another poem there was a hiatus in meaning between lines, which I filled by in-serting the word "trees," which was already in the vocabulary of the poem. There are no other important changes of words.

I have omitted from the book over forty poems which were either incomplete, fragmentary, or immature. Otherwise this book contains all the poems from the manuscripts placed in my hands. I have found references to a few others, mostly written in childhood, which appear to have been lost. Two of the poems have previously been published: "Orpheus" in *Decision,* and "Even the Gulls of the Cool Atlantic" in *Chimera.*

In arranging the poems, I have partly grouped them by subject, partly tried to place them in an order that would be interesting and readable. In some places there is a sequence and development of thought running through several poems.

Miss Murray titled very few of her poems. When she did, I have used her title. For most of the others, I have used the first line or part of it. Occasionally I have used a phrase from some other part of the poem, very rarely a descriptive title of my own.

New York, 1946

GRANT CODE

CONTENTS

BOOK THREE

BOOK FOUR

BOOK FIVE

BOOK SIX

BOOK SEVEN

BOOK ONE

IF HERE IN THE CITY

IF, here in the city, lights glare from various source,
  Look out of the window, thin-faced man.
Three portent cities repeat the pattern and the course
That history ran.

Three slender veins, clotted and ambiguous,
Are those inlocked hands.
Three startled cries now rise incredulous,
Where once sprang barren sands.

Give back night to receding sky.
Let stars (the things that remain)
Orbit their quiet to the lie
That is here city and various city pain.

AS IT SHOULD BE

DO not say the cluttered mass upheaped about the street
   Is not as it should be,
Or the rows and squares and blare of passing objects
Not as it should be.
Paris, New York, London and the meeting on Fleet Street,
The heat, the smell and its ill effects.
Who then objects?

In the spring I have my land, the crocus coming up.
There is complaining as there is wind!
Sitting in the morning and the evening,
Complaining, as there is wind.
A woman with unpinned hair, a moaning dog, to disrupt
The moderate time, the sleepers, weaving
Inevitable evening.

A million clocks will talk out across the city,
And all things on the run,
And people angle on about the day,
The ugly baggage, and the cripple—always the cripple!
Things on the run,
With us who are the other people, the neat, the sly, the witty,
Crisp or drab, the small child with its apple,
The men who bit and knew the face of Eve's tart-surfaced
   apple,
And then again the cripple.

ONE MORGANATIC LEER

YOU think you complain of the ugliness of people.
   Meet your own bed.
Smell what you said.
Your words, unmitigated, dead,
Sink like a noon sun in the crass tomb beneath the steeple.

Two feet above the sand, look down
A tartan shore,
A clan, a clack, a whore,
A mobile open door,
To the dog against the tree, the brittle mugging clown.

Claws like tumbled fingers here
Stand for hands,
Elastic bands,
Minds and trends.
Thighs sprout here enough to breed the honor of your mor-
   ganatic leer.

A SMALL TALE WITH INTERRUPTIONS

THERE'S a small tale I'd like to tell you here, a bit sad, I
believe.

NOT TOO SAD

There was a little man. And his actions must be jerked
By a series of mental strings and attitudinizings.
He used to go to a small little pub somewhere near Whitehall.
Down a drear dark street when his wage came to him he would
go
And there he would imbibe the raw stuff and rub his hands
willy . . .

WILLY NILLY

And clatter his feet on the floor, not speaking or lifting his eyes,
But living in a strange and bell-clear world of his own
Till the hour struck home.

WHY? AND WHY?

Why, if he hadn't, he would have risen
Each morning with the blank walls and the bleak yard moan-
ing at him
And he would have said to himself, "How wise I am . . .

(A CHUCKLE)

"What shades and pleasantries my life must possess.
I must thank all the high swing of things for the clock that
ticks,
The drip of the tap and the sound of the kettle
That whistles up my shilling's gas and whistles up my tea too.
Look, here's the bread, and here's the fine limp book I've read.
Oh, I'm a sensible fellow and a practical bit of a lad.
I'm not dead to gentle satire; for I'm conscious of the other me,
And smile and sigh away these anthropological shortcomings."

"I can hear and see and cull the meats.
And I am at least three quarters alive to the wonders of the
    Space-Moulder and Star-Spinner,
Where he leans, checkmating the irrelevant with the irrever-
    ent . . .

THE SEED WITH INFINITY

"I'm so sensible that I simply won't be ·. . . Oh, won't be . . .
    Oh, will not be."
(Here the little man leaped up and down, though he had the
    black hat and black gloves on.)

I BELIEVE THE DAY WAS SUNDAY

Sunday, you, now! He might have cried out in the dark street
A thousand rilling years. This was his dream,
To break through himself, to do something beautifully.
That was against the turn of the very stars which knew the
    reality
Of the lightest of his piped illusions.
He would sit down thoughtfully afterward. "It was wrong to
    do that."
(Here he'd chuff his hands together.)
"Or rather, indeed, how very calm I feel! A simple innocence
    holds me;
For verily, I was proclaimed an angel. I saw the little gods
Stirring themselves in their own sweet day, after beds."

But the truth was that the poor little devil had been run over,
Dead in the street in his Sunday best.

STUDY FOR AN EAST SIDE BALLAD

THREE men sat at a millstone table.
   One looked up, one down, one about,
And they were one head and a fable.
Spin the millstone, spin the millstone out!

For the mind of the men spoke in it.
As the millstone were they themselves all-wise.
The large and the small of them sit
With skinny elbows and backs that fall and rise.

.   .   .

They played by the water . . . Chuck, Mink, Stode.
And the fat Jew fellow with the nose
Strutted the glitter of a wagon-load—
Pink, striped, candied, lemon, froze.

Up by the Avenue east, river junk—
Old shops, a dirt-colored cabbage-king,
Eating bread and eating cheese in one big hunk.
Old Pasqual', cabbage-king, breaks into swing.

Play by the water, Chuck, Mink, Stode,
River-ratlets with rail-thin thighs.
Sandy-haired, bandy-kneed Stode,
White trousers flapping, gob hat, sea eyes.

Sandy Sam on leave on land!
Old man sits in the sun and blinks,
Strokes his beard, and his son's been canned,
Pulls at the yellow-white threads and thinks.

And the sandy young fellow and the Jew
And the cabbage-king of the Avenue east . . .

They don't know, but himself, he knew
What it's like to be old like a rabbi priest.

As they breathe out and in at the table,
All the energies of a lifetime's thought
On the weight of an object and analyzed fable
Bundle in hard knotty thoughts in this spot.

Chuck, Mink, Stode run from the river
Over to Second and Third and the shop.
"Ikey!" and "Ikey!" and "Give us a silver!"
Or bread from Pasquale, with a handspring and hop.

All home to supper, Chuck, Mink, Stode.
Fine fat Jew fellow looks at the sun.
Up with the glitter-gilt, on with the load.
Young Mister Sandy Sam off to meet the Hon'.

Pasqual', cabbage-king, garlic in the nose,
Off for a great spaghett', turns to close up,
Hurries the shutter down, takes the apron from the clothes.
Old man sits rocking, in his small black hat.
Old man sits rocking, sipping at a cup.
Old man sits rocking in the dusk.

DREAMS OF A MODERN ARCHITECT:
I. GOTHIC

THE oblique chapels of the Gothic
 Blink with a dim prenatal distinction.
The querulous beam, championing through the thick
Spumy scent, quibbles with the dark in some elation.

And the passions of night are out,
And the slippery imp chuckles at eaves
Where the moss-staled gargoyles let the useful spout
Of mouth suck in thirst and then relieve.

The devil and the flesh spank thighs,
Duck from sight and torture down the aisle,
Mangle the accosting prayers and sighs,
Heightening the drab pale monks, each in his militant file.

The in and out of God has lapped such vital tears,
And now the necromancers and mongolian apes
Tear at the crisp blue air and use their fears
For bolts and doors, their skins for capes.

Within the niche, the sterile-eyed Madonna screened,
Apostles, chipped and overdressed,
But lovely in the meaning of preened
Undulating beards, all abundantly and well blessed.

Mongoloid fool, your saffron seasick face
Will do its harm to women and to children,
A fangy slit-eyed creature of no race,
Perversion from true fact, with natural spleen for men.

In the chapel they will nurture and condone you,
Put you in striped pants and high fool's hat,

24

Teach sordid pity and lust in the more than casual few,
Then gibber and bang your blunt hands flat

Against the inundated void that is more devil,
More sucking pity, black, sleep-tasting.
Gothic chapels watch the steeple; the squinting gargoyles spill
Fools bred in the aisles that somnolent monks are strictly cas-
    trating.

DREAMS OF A MODERN ARCHITECT:
II. STARVED HOUSES

THE starved houses, without bricks or people,
   Wander about the desolate streets.
Little boys would have stained their corners yellow
And old wives cherished their stoops.

The architect counts his ribs, the house its bone.
The window frames distant emphatic day, concave night.
The attempt to shape and lay the air is done.

It is the young architect in the old village,
And with what trepidity he reaches for a time,
Dizzy with starved action, handles clay,
Threads with the slightest over-dream a city
Planned with a bird upon each bough, a light upon each face.

The neat Sunday family directs its walk toward church.
The airplane and lark comment upon the weather.
From each home, a Jove, springs its living wisdom.
Old men with pipes click dry thumbs on round bowls.

The nightmare of empty houses in retreat,
The lovely unwanted, with drafting board on his knee,
Glares at the grave placement of nursery and kitchen,
Measuring each with the fragile scale of starved necessity.

The dog lopes through and squats beside the fire.
And there is a place for good wine and for pacing,
And working his plans and prints and city tower.
The unemployed architect employed in tomorrow's tracing.

THE BUILDER

"IT is the action of water that is the nearest thing to man,"
That is what the young of the people cried, lifting their
Heads from the work they had turned to with indolence.

"Crack at that pile, young fellow!" went up the sullen cry.
"No time to stop in the work and the job, only time to breathe,
And breathe in your own fine sweat, for the mountain air's too
    good
For a world to stop us for, us for, us for!"

That's how it goes in life, while the seasons churn past your
    eyes:
High scuttle of dying leaves in fall like a stab and a stain,
The color of words that are dreamed in the head,
And spring prancing up like a dainty colt,
Picking the place for its feet, and lilies work up from its feet.

There are heaps of green everywhere, everywhere, and the shift
    of leaves.
The quick goat butts his mate,
And the ram putters out a stammering bleat,
Like a song that falls on its heels,
Where we should be with our mate, and we aren't, we aren't.
Oh, we aren't, we aren't, we aren't.

I want to wander over the hills and down to the water,
And if there is sea I want to pack it up in my arms,
And let the blue globe of all the wide water fill my mouth
Till my jaw hangs loose, and come piling into me,
Fill up my head, my chest, and the sea-filled loins to burst in
    me.

"Crack at that pile, young fellow," went up the sullen cry.
"We're building towers of Babel that will crumble down before
    dawn,
Like the falling of water down and down to the sea,
And we'd die making towers of Babel while they tumble down
    to the sea."

THE RIVETER'S HELPER

THE man who smiles and totters with the riveter,
   Throws the red rivet through the paupered air,
Is more than the simple statement or young inventor,
Glaring with spectacles from the brain's cramped lair.

He waves a hand with its brisk intelligible symbol.
The facts are his children, not the plan.
His wife has a face as still as the grave upon the knoll
Where the women clap and stand to wait for every man.

Twirling between girders and the night,
The man who smiles like dawn and lights the cigarette
Nods to another day and wishes for a child of his delight.
A quick reflex admits the brawn, the brain the infant intellect.

LULLABY

SLEEP, little architect. It is your mother's wish
That you should lave your eyes and hang them up in
dreams.
Into the lowest sea swims the great sperm fish.
If I should rock you, the whole world would rock within my
arms.

Your father is a greater architect than even you.
His structure falls between high Venus and far Mars.
He rubs the magic of the old and then peers through
The blueprint where lies the night, the plan the stars.

You will place mountains too, when you are grown.
The grass will not be so insignificant, the stone so dead.
You will spiral up the mansions we have sown.
Drop your lids, little architect. Admit the bats of wisdom into
your head.

NIGHT RISING FROM SLEEK COILS

NIGHT rising from sleek coils, a snake in the house of the
    Architect,
And the breath of the sleeper rising, and the window where
    the leaves gather,
And the insect repeating in sound the monotonous stillness the
    stars inflict
Upon the changeable vision of the night mind and its flutter.

In the hour when the Mother has become an eye in sleep,
Over the palm of the cold the woman stirs, and it is her own
    hand.
She draws to all the breathing leaves the deep
Sea tone that moans their tired weight, their salt beginning and
    ultimate end.

The woman tugs from the scent what the memory of space in-
    tends
Only to be grasped by those who are white with time and tide,
And she expands into the City, where the wall extends
Both up and down, and yet seems neither narrow, high, nor
    wide.

The house of the Architect and the archaic symbols of the dark
Cry for the dance of the wandering optimism.
O stir, with your memory of a stark
Hand opening like a flower upon the mock action of rock
    cataclysm.

BOOK TWO

WORK IN PROGRESS

LOOK to your hands, life of rare genuflection!
    The wind works a strange destruction
Upon leaves of trees. And look to your feet:
Where walking is done, the winter cares little about the neat
Step. And look to all that is yours,
So that we who will to possess may not call you ours.

Learn, from the indifference of the land,
To draw back from the drooped lids and the wavering demand.
A child's face is a peculiar thing where it does not belong!
What mature mind would turn to a wrong
Act? Therefore look to your hills and your sun:
Gather beside the walks and the ways where the wild deer run.

THERE ARE SHAPES OUT OF THE NORTH

THERE are shapes out of the north.
    That you are of the prow of the iceland;
That your face is the Kelt and the North,
As the race and brief shore's hard-swept sand.

Brittle spoors of the sea in strange environment,
That is your step; a colloquial murmur, that is your being.
Scud, then, from the obsolete into a new wind's abandonment,
Or cut at the sea-sperm calculated to draw you into
A nightmare's scheming.

Only remember this:—of all things that tread well,
You tread splendidly along the route.
Earth and tide, age of the mountain, the lift and swell:
These are the shapes of you the waves dispute.

YOU TALK OF ART

YOU talk of art, of work, of books.
    Have you ever sat down, thought all that's to do?
That book to read, that book to write,
Sat down, stood up, walked back and forth,
Because not an action you could do would
Fill the gap that's wanting action to the chin?

Look. Look into the past one damned moment,
And on that you ask me to work, to dream, to do?
Try it yourself on nothing. I can't.

Every confounded one has had so much of life
That left them gasping in a stinking or a lighter air,
Left out of breath and glad to think at last,
Higher or lower, their there and there and there.

And where am I? Where I began, and where I'll end:
Sitting, sitting, with the last grain of will
Rotting in time, and there's no time or tide in me.

You talk of art, of work, of books.
I'll talk of nothing in its lowest state,
Talk till my jaw hangs limply at the joint,
And the talk that's one big yawn in the face of all of you,
Empty as head, empty as mood, and weak.
And I can hear all the watery wells of desolation
Lapping a numbing sleep within the head.

WHAT CAN I DO, METHUSELAH?

WHAT can I do, Methuselah? Your time is mine,
    Without reason, but with flattened sheets,
Sheets wrapping corpses, or sheet sky,
White, with that blue tired undertone,
I am here, with arms, arms asking without voice;
For voices cannot always say something from the middle,
From the stomach that is empty, or even lift lips.
Delicate crescent lips cannot speak so loudly,
But only mute when all the heart has driveled out.
And, oh, I am here alone, now it has all the birds
In flutter and in knell-curved distances.
What to say, what to say, that only arms can say it?
Wrap corpses in a shroud of cooler evening sky,
Corpses of even shrouded illusion, as is emptiness.
Look here where with cherry-colored scarfs
I wrap my mistress' thoughts, with wider arms,
Rolling her eyes upon my outstretched palms,
Till the hours grow, and the low-flung beard of night
Has wedged itself between another mood.
Down the thousand years, you shuffle back the corridors,
Measuredly twist a pale-rimmed curve of the lips.
What can I do, Methuselah, without the wisdom
Of your laughter?
Give me a cockerel heaven, so that I may crow
To the turn of your rising smile.
Reflect the half-ripple of your features and be still?
Or raise my arms higher till the pearls have dropped?

ASCETIC: TIME MISPLACED

DRIVE your rod with a consistence down,
  Striking the cold black loam,
Till with a flourish and a sudden cry,
The thin strand of infinitesimal leaf!
(Stark in its beginning as a simple touch,
Made to feel about the splendid earth,
Palming the hand down there and everywhere)
One infinitesimal leaf leaps up!

I have seen hills, and the rhythm
Will not leave my head.
I have seen—since I was a pink and cottoned
Little thing—
Leaves with the brimming sun spilt down.
I have thought myself into Pan
And run with Sappho after women's feet,
Hated the stuff that makes all life,
For the very slough and insect breed of it.
I have made the asses of the flatlands bray,
Kicking their hooves up in the thistled brake,
Dreamed to drink with gods, and puttered
In a frenzy with those less than mortal.
I have dreamed and dreamed myself to life
And back again.
And now with my body fat, my brain irresolute,
I see nothing once again, but nothing!
Only the bloom of an impeccably quiet dust!

THEY SAY

IF I had spent whole nights watching you,
  Gutting the candles in so many winks,
I should be Pharisee or utter hypocrite,
Whichever pleased to put your mind at ease.

I call myself illusion all transgressional.
(There's little pity rollicked here for me.)
I know the very truth of action is at surface,
A string pulled in the outward throw of things.

By Heaven, take the cake! I'll take one too!
Lecherous thoughts and puritanical rub grey;
But never mind—even if the grey's the basis for decline—
We'll take the cake, and swim the Hellespont of time!
And if my Hellespont should be a gutter-swell,
Remember me to Lucifer!

But come, there's so much rot in that collapse;
For what am I but I, whether the conscience
Turns to mud or passes to a more ambiguous state?
I shall be I, quite still beside the night,
Dreaming Samaritan, rolling little pills of wax
Dropped by the candles . . . and the hours.

EGO ALTER EGO

I AM watching you as you stand,
A child of riddles in the head,
Of thoughts that rill in circles,
Big and little, pricked with doubt,
The fault turned always in.

What I could do or say lies here,
In my smile, and in my anger,
In my wonder at your consciousness
That always answers every why
With an ironic answering smile,
Twisting the full flesh of your lips.

Stand before me. Let down your lids.
Now let your body lean against
The warm afternoon rocks.
Listen to the slavering of the waves,
Mouthing along the shore,
And feel that I am respectable,
Here where I lie, my body naked,
My sharp imprint in the shadow;
That I am an independent void,
Absorbing into my wisdom and my mind
All that you have to give in words,
Hoping in the simplicity of my listening
That you may forget eternal self.

We scrambled down these rocks together,
And your eyes were blue candor circles,
Child's eyes, and enigmatic for me.
I wondered if this was you
When, looking up, I saw you looking down,
You, without place or sex,

Quiet, and with the first clear idea,
Awakening to yourself with wings.
The swoop of a gull swinging out
In one wide taking had caught you,
And you were that quiet nothingness.

One could put up one's hand
And grasp the hollow glass of the sky,
Rattling the gulls against the sides,
And the screech of their cry,
Flipping them back and forth,
Like motes of pollen on the wind
Without end and without beginning.

Oh, the benevolence of space!
It has the graciousness of motherhood,
The full breast and the suckling,
And the man against her knees,
The great abstract growth of space.

We are so young, you and I.
People, pointing, whisper amongst themselves
"Too young, too young, for such an age!"
And then like rubble rumbling down
The embankment to splash noisily,
They shake their heads,
All, "Child, child, eternal child!"
And so the river carries on the words,
We are so young, you and I.

And our childhood is our past,
And our future indomitably shadowing
The pits black and maligned
And beyond the dustbowls,

Even the gold dust stings, or so they say,
Stings in the very strength . . . disillusion.

Harness that star before it slips.
It is the bone of mind,
The will to concrete life that you have left,
Dust in the eyes, the nose.
Bury yourself in sterility of purpose
But tell me while you follow this down and down.

But, come, stand before me; speak.
Stand where the sun is warmest,
A pile of shells, dusk-mauve, rose-fluted,
And I am gone with your thoughts of me.
Stir the conglomerate brew of memory,
The day of reckoning . . . an insidious pool.

YOU, HELD IN THE THIN CUSP
OF THE NIGHT

YOU, held in the thin cusp of the night,
  Capped by unevenly placed stars,
Rocking yourself like a blonde char, knowing tomorrow's labor,
Or today's soldier, as he shouts, and mars
The sleek dragon, having been put to flight
Once too often, before its enigmatic horror.

Turrets of words and words the structure of your head;
Grammatical sense a wide web;
Coolness and fragility barely giving life to the somehow dead,
Somehow dead, knowing its second nature to be more ebb
Than flow, more go than come; and yet to come must go . . .
All that is river, be it high or low.

Lift your hair up to stand between the fingers,
Touching knowledge of leaves, anatomy, dark hours.
Not so much energy lies there as potential energy,
Not so much of tree and flower as their potential powers—
Ideas of people, pennies to tired singers,
Whose fluctuant song haunts out the young man's memory.

These acts, fears and several vices,
"I am I's" that stand alone or chance a stranger's careless dice,
Raise for a race such paralytic voices
As God has become used to and men hear in white mice.
Typist fingers strike your hair, use unscabbarded pen;
For idiot's age or virulent time must succumb to deep mute
    men.

Look at the shallow surface and be granite and limbed body.
Swing more than adder tongue or mother feeling.
With hands that are unringed unsoft and slender,

43

In heart be the thing that flexes before leaping.
Lean at your city window, as rounded sun to sea,
And though mind is act between shadow and shadow,
Night shall admit its subtle shadower.

We have seen you look as a man with strange possibilities,
As a child with odd angularity, and slumped;
And we have and have not denied you your sensitiveness.
We have seen you on fields humped
And at various leisure reaching for flowers that we knew,
And turning with nervous fingers shells upon rocks we knew.

London streets and bus tickets snapped in Piccadilly,
With the soot and the wind and the rain let loose:
There we have watched you amble by without maturity,
Pushing back hair from thoughts on land that killed the goose
Destined to lose the golden egg, this island that we knew,
This river, this Embankment, this power for the few.

No more may you know from your window
Than you have stroked, heard or broken
In the days and hours of your pain.
Your mind, now flexed and lean in archives of the spoken,
Must choose between the slant Sphynx whose head the sands
    repudiate and blow
And the wide hurt that shows dark flowers after rain.

THE YOUNG HOST OF ROCKLEDGE

OVER Saranac, even the lights have gone:
  The dark guests flick silver candles with a star.
Over the sparsely peopled town, the narcotic snow, one
Strange unseen figure after another puts out its hand far
To the crackling rim of the mountain and breaks bread.
The wind for a brief moment sniffs the snow of sleep,
Blowing it high to the sterile sleek sky of the winter dead.
The multitudes of two and two keep
Watch in the slender shape of birch and hemlock and the larch.
Quietly we each nibble at the corner of a different thought.
The woman, lovely as all things must be, sits with the terrible
    march
Of the insect and the stars within her head forever caught,
Forever bound by the delicate web of the hidden spider.
The man, the host, smiling because it is not too easy, turns
    about,
Until we see the oblique church figured in the eyes and mask
    of the everlasting newcomer.
A hand, across the face and lids, shakes out
And down onto the table the still New England dust.
The guests nod, whispering between the unblown flames.
Far beyond night, the vacant quiet turns from its space—
    absorbing lust
To answer the queries of a little child and play the glad old
    games.

We see the real host of the house and why the tall trees stand;
And the unseen guests draw three full seas of laughter from the
    eye:
"The son of the house demands a silver snow upon a summer
    strand!"
What has been brooding in a faithless sleep leaps from the table
    with a thin bird's-cry.

AS THE SUMMER SUN COMES DOWN INTO THE AUTUMN TREES

For Dai

AS the summer sun comes down into the autumn trees,
     And we feel the hills to be drums between the knees
Of the phlegmatic Indian depositing his thought by beat,
As we advance under the birch and hemlock or retreat
With our factual minds hunting the winter place,
I think we would not forget our one brief act in space.

The mathematical scar has alarmed or delighted us.
We break with many fingers the uncertain truce
Between the ledge and the vegetable earth,
Dividing our appetites according to their worth.
Somewhere the satisfaction lies in the shy animal,
A moment touching grass, the next leaping the enigmatic wall.

We cannot incantate without the leaves or the wind.
We could not turn to each other with crying at an end
Or make the gesture of the mind a fact,
If we had not conceived of the extraordinary act
That recurs like the wandering race, the day and season,
And the woman who forever hums the name of an unnatural
     son.

The terrible legend, disporting with the night,
Sends the birch and pine in tiers of shivering flight
Over the climate of the hills descending to the valley;
While we remain all quiet in that remarkable memory,
Our minds extending through a fragmentary space
To grasp the implication of the drum that speaks the thought
Of the inverted face.

HERE WE STAND BEFORE THE TEMPORAL WORLD

HERE we stand before the temporal world,
  And whether we care to cast our minds
Or shiver from our words all that refutes
The clarity of thought . . .
Whether we wish to deflect the rudiments of source
. . . Bare bastard brats in summing up the whole . . .
These things I do not know.

Words have been to me like steps
Revolving and revolving in one cell.
Perhaps others have felt the limits of the pendulum,
Looking to the vast confines of night,
And conscious only of the narrow head,
The brief skull imminent of life,
Gray granules that, like Time, run through the hours.

Caesar walked quietly in his garden.
Two scribes walked gravely at his side.
The smooth pink marble of the fluted column passed
Reminded him of warm wine from the grapes,
The glitter of a spear dropped carelessly,
And caught by a hand quicker than he could see
Its slanting fall,
Reminded him of the shallow eyes that glinted
As he passed between two worlds, their own and his.
His thoughts tended toward irrelevance,
But his words cut out the veriest patterns
Of an eastern drive toward the steeples of far Babylon.

YOU SPOKE OF WINDMILLS

IT is Quixotic to be fighting windmills.
    In my inevitable surrealism, not even hills
Could be more than the narrow edge of illusion;
Nor my fat Panza donkey-sitting to the exclusion
Of anything but donkey-sitting.

Always a gilt knight against a plumed sky,
A malleable reference in the sense to "cap-a-pie,"
A Dulcinea to facilitate the soul.
And thus one struts down time's declining role;
Even if tomorrow is, while yesterdays move out.

You spoke of windmills where the mind degrades;
You clipped your words with the worth that truth engraves.
Yet know the vast aloneness of this Don,
A querulous soldier, a life's inveterate pawn,
As sensible in his brave dream as we are not.

BOOK THREE

THE LONG TRAIL

I HAVE been marking the long high roads.
  I think it was over the trail
That angles on, riddling the mountain wood,
Up and down in the cool musk valleys,
Up and up to the height, where, blue and drawn,
The reaches and the farther hills
Turned their great shadows and grave lines
To more than form, to more than opulent color.

THREE MOUNTAINS HIGH

THREE mountains high:
  Oh, you are a deep and marvelous blue!
It was with my palms
That I rounded out your slopes;
There was an easy calmness,
An irrelevant ease, that touched me,
And I stretched my arms and smoothed
Three mountains high.

THINGS THAT ARE SINUOUS

THINGS that are sinuous are the rivers of the land—
   Women stalking, with the ripple of cats
Along the leg, and movements of the body
In deep eddies, in silk transparencies.

Rivers of the tumbled slopes,
The flatlands to the west,
Tidal rivers, licking and drawing back,
The whole weight of protuberance toward the sea,
Marking a salt ridge in the bright flush of the flats.

They are women with bare and subtle feet,
Of brooks, of rills, of mountain lakes,
Of turbulent cascades, of torrential moments,
Of long coiled tenuous drift, with one still cloud
Sucking from rim to rim of that insoluble thing . . .
Down to the river and the beat of the river.

NOT THAT I HAD EVER LAUGHED TOO MUCH

NOT that I had ever laughed too much
  Beside the million-mile looped river,
Turning its course with slug trepidity
Toward my dangled fingers.
I came to smile berserkly at the dawn,
Forcing myself to lie beside this river,
Shaping a pocket in the shrill damp air
To warm my sides along.
Now even the smile has gone, and I am face to face
With the insoluble riddle of the moment,
Hold myself empty, and mistily reflected
In the jade gray water.
River them, river whole times to sensation,
Water dip-dipping to the finger tips,
And in the touch a bird's diminuendo transcendental,
Masticated in the new reality.
I came to smile at dawns because I thought it just.
Now I momently relieve such strain
By throwing back my lids to free my eyeballs,
Relaxing the body to strain perception.
God, river your thoughts; I'll river mine, and here
There's nothing to ask but clouds about the head,
Wind-winnowed grasses in the hair, and blown
Down the stirring water,
More finely felt, more apparent to nuance,
That is the finite shading which reveals the whole,
Now smiling and now laughing beside the stream of river,
Exquisitely conscious of the self-advent.

LIKE A WIND PASSING SLOWLY ALONG THE VALLEY

LIKE a wind passing slowly along the valley,
   That which passes by is narrow, and is the woman,
Is the autumn leaf, leaping between one tree
And the long looning of a bird, to scan
One tree, one land, one river in no hour.

Pools, where evening leaves rattle fan-whipped
On water, on the backs of tilting drakes,
And in the dry throat unmossed of up-ripped
Up-leached rocks . . . pools that gather into lakes
In a locked world whose blue hills edge between.

So down to the treed dark plain from height,
Like a wind passing slowly along the valley;
So many women move Indian-eyed and light
From far walking and knowledge swept up freely.

DROUGHT

DROUGHT, what inscrutable mask!
   Over the fragile, over the musk—
Over all these green hills
That once filled their sides and valleys
With innumerable lacerate pools.
Fish with their tails unminted,
Their silver surface hollowed,
Under the spring's flood stones,
Over the rumpled dry stream,
Their bones laced to the bed
And mouths V'd wide unbreathing.

THE EXILES

THE day we stood as people stand
   Looking out toward the land,
We were lovers of things beyond our bodies.

We were grave women, simple men;
With less than a turn we knew it then—
A place, a land, a cliff as silver as bitten sea.

Without a stir, we straddled our minds
Into remembered outer rinds—
River and height and outflanked shore.

The long keen stride on the plow-churned earth
Meant with the pain the full year's birth
While seasons like boys spat seeds against our knees.

SPRING

OH, but there is a laughing Spring
With its head back and its mouth wide,
Square breasts and masculine swing
In every leap and stride.

There is a mountain of energy
In the drop and flair of spray:
That is tomorrow, not torrid lethargy;
Not whimpering April, but tumultuous May.

Willows snap the too-smoothed slope;
The birch knifes through the night;
The lilies shout within their fragile scope
And every trace of sweet is put to flight.

Sap flies high to the head of tall
Trees in a leaping drunk from Winter's
Tattered leaves, embittered fall,
Ice to the bone, to the life, in jagged splinters.

Spring, the cudgel, flaying soft the land,
Swaggers all-world-wide across the sky,
Lifting waves from sea to the hard bruised sand,
Laughing earth, abrupt from the wake of things that die.

IMPROVISATION FOR SPRING

OH, but there is a laughing Spring!
  Even the little men see that:
A running through white board towns singing,
A light that glints from painted steeples,
A minnow-silver rain
Of all the clouds contain.

Spring, cracking its buds,
Every instant a remark,
Each brisk spanked cloud that scuds
A brief "Out!" for the invulnerable sun;
The sea in May
A barking ivory spray.

These are total energies.
Spring is not soft, but direct.
It is only the by-play that has its lethargies.
The life stamps and commands.
It is the little man
Who tricks his little span.

VERMONT: THE HILLS AND
THE VALLEYS

TREMENDOUS are the ways of the simple people:
The hills speak with their mouths;
The sky laughs out of the rims of their eyes.
The earth walks with the feet of the people;
And the wind and the dead are their souls awake;
And the sleep that is theirs comes when the eyelid
Slips down to meet the soiled slant of their cheeks.

Great are the mountain slopes curving along the line
Flanked by the river or the smooth glint of the track of the
        train:
A speed of smoke, a sprung coil loosely heaped.
Look to the right, look to the left and the fields
That fit in languid patterns between the trees,
Umber cornstalks, hay in warmth-spilt stacks.

Tight is the hair of women who call cows to the milking:
Wrists and fingers play out the movement of the udder-press.
White is the angle and the hiss and splash of milk.

The oxen plow and wagon the hay in its high dung-gold,
Making long horns shape and hold the moon,
The red of their sides squat.
The trees spring in wide green waves to the wind,
To the fields and the well-palmed spread of space.

The men are before the night,
The cracks of their cheeks filled with dust,
And the hands heavy like listless rakes hung down,
And the dirt and sweat on their lips,
And the lift and fall of their chests.

Steps of men and women go from the field to the home,
From the plow to the reaping in the deep high swell of wheat.

These are the simple people,
Whose hands rest still on a Sabbath.
And great are the fields and the mountains,
And great are the slopes and the valleys.

VERMONT JOURNEY

MOMENTARY lift of plain and sea,
    Rib of land and then the sea.
Oh, the immense sea-rock, the land!
O Land that in back time
Moved beyond waves' mad leap or suck,
Deep suck, mouthing rivers!
Plainly the rivers running through
Gutted these cool green throats of valleys.

Blue Ridge men move their
Slow lean limbs on alien ground,
Muttering with the strange tongue
Of careful-witted people.
Alien men, a mountain of the east!
Yet ax is sound, a lilting ring
To those who lift and strike it clean
On alien or any other land.

   "Men are women!"
The old thinned beards fade.
Evening leaves only the circle of porch sitters
With their short-napped beards,
Slow-moving satyr strands.
   "Trees flesh to the boy."
He lifts his hand soft,
Like a woman drawing tears,
Down and away from his face.
When the leaves fall, he weeps
With the eyes of an old woman.

Great flung and measureless steps
And a woman running along,
A dog twisting and pacing at her feet.

She is running dryly with the dog,
Her eyes cutting on beyond the river.
A cool stare through the half dusk,
She meets the memory of the day,
The profit of the milking with its loss.

What tales are linked up in this land!
But mountains and the people are equally grave
And the best that's said is brief.

OLD MEN

THE corn is ripe.
    I HAVE known the heat to come up a smoke-pot.
The corn is ripe.
I have put out my hand and plucked grass,
Put the grass in my mouth and chewed a cud,
Spat the cud high in the air,
And hit the field lily smack in the center.
Couldn't do better than that!

        There was sea here:
If I breathe deep I can still smell salt earth.
I found two twisted sea-copias once;
I was a boy, and I remember how bleached they looked,
Cool in my earth-stained hand.

        The hay's rust.
The sun is like a quick sore running.
There should be green hay.
The underside of water is the color I saw.
I used to gather it in great handfuls,
And pluck at the soft green beards,
Chew at the narrow grass-stalks.

        When I was a boy
I used to go naked in the quarries,
Lift the great white slabs to me.
The sun beat hard on my muscles, drummed the rhythm,
And there was a fine wide sea-surge in my head:
White marble glare and the glow of my young smooth skin.
        But I was a boy then.

Rain in the mountains; rain in the hills:
The cows are moaning late these nights!

Rain in the mountains; rain in the hills:
The cows are moaning late these nights.
The cows moan still before morning.

NEW ENGLAND WOMAN

THE tall dark sharp-faced woman came to the door
   And gave the mop a crack across the rail of the porch.
A dry leaf zigzagged down between two maples
And blew with a dry crisp patter on the street.

The morning had been clear like honey.
And now the autumn sun spilt down, amber deep,
And warm about the near trees and the far blue hills.

She would have liked rain and the long black drizzled days,
When the trees were bare, with the last sad leaf turned
A little patterned skeleton on the ground,
And there was the cold sleet feeling in the air
That seemed to hold the land,
When the trees were awkward bony things
Straggling up to a far-off stretch of sky,
And there was the smallest etch of a crow's black wing
And the shrill cracked cry.

These were the times and feelings that were made
Of the same stuff as her pale face, coiled black hair,
The sharpness of her joints and the brooding of her mood.

She gave the mop another crack and went inside.

MAD JOHN

THE John rolled back where he was,
   Grinned a corn-row of teeth at the sky.
The light was a pink mouse run off its feet,
Streaming its tail and winding to the sea.
The John sat grinning out about him,
Flapping his hands, squashed pink on green.
"What did I come for? What did I seen? Uh?"
The words plunked and rubbed back into silence.
If the crow had squawked out to him, maybe . . .
Or a jittering chatter of things had spoken . . .
(And spoken out of turn in the wide big flow!)
But nothing'd answer if he didn't care.
            And he didn't!

The John is a dull yellow-matted head of a lad;
Rolled back to the ground, he's lying,
With tobacco smoke in his lung, and a cob.
He's snorting down the wind, letting go smoke.
And where'll it go to when it meets the night,
Comes up to night and joins the swell of black?
The John shrugs, smacks the green, and turns.
All the great weight of him goes round.
(And all the hills shrugged before time and him!)
"What did I come for? What did I seen? Uh?"
He'd ask and turn again to grab the first quiet shakedown of
      stars.
He'd have said and seen more than cob-smoke,
If he'd wanted to!
That's what he said.

THE MAGDALINA

THEY had stood expostulating to their God,
   They with their shallow-pool eyes,
Catching the web-grey sky between their thoughts,
Across the fields, with the endless slabs of soil
Turned to the light and the icy pools eyed up.
These men stared, mumbling in bleak stolidity.

I slumped against the drift fence where I stood,
One lean hand had squared with work about the fingers.
Hands of poets stood out from my arms beside them.
These standing men, with incorrigible fists,

The seed of grey swung women, grew to life
Up from the shallow hollows of the land,
Long gaunt strides of the indefatigable land-born,
Well-tempered females, breast and spanned hip swung.

The hung sky sagged toward the higher rise,
Pressing the last echo of a breath beyond the field.
The cold arched and stiffened out to the horizon.

A woman was fingering her sides through red cloth.
Her hands dreamed from the wrist in slender threads,
While the tall gaunt women spread their skirts against her.
The wide mute spread strode strongly with its men,
Marking away the far bells' sullen beat.

The woman shoved the red cloth from her face.
I turned, for the sun had circled the bent sky,
Leaving me in my own shadow, so that I must turn
And turn again to face her.
"My name is Magdalina and my sides and the sun and forever."
That is where the rivered summer wheat has tangled,
The concentrated desolation of a span.

Into the cloudless smooth of space, the bells
Sounded like grey skirts fluttering to mind.
The men are standing with bared eyes curled along pages;
The women, with the fine weight of their hips in place,
Rock imperceptibly to the high chant of a hymn.

Here there is nothing:
The fence, the mud, the fields dragged stark and undulate,
A few dried leaves whirled red.

TALK OF PEOPLE IN WARNING

WE are the green torrents invulnerable;
    We are an admixture of trees and black earth.
Sundays come in dark cloth, and all weeks end.
Fishing smacks from Hyste to Perth
Flatter the sea
With its immensity.

We plow, we back up the day to breaking.
Sackcloth and ashes! Sackcloth and ashes!
Not uncomplaining widows on Sunday.
Not now. Never now. A woman dashes,
Squats in pain,
Remains in pain.

We are faces blackening windows,
Eyes that pass through stone and remember
Sands that number us, brisk stars to perceive
From the dry-boned November
The seed of us,
Tremulous.

THE SONG OF THINGS WATCHING

DO you see the lovers?
    We see quiet trees together
Where young men knelt, flowers
Where young girls stood, daughters
Of earth-winding water.

The old father plucks
With the hands of a dry wind.
The old mother clucks,
A soft tongue, with the rooks
Of sleep intent upon her mind.

Love reaching night
Stands slender-hipped,
Slender-fingered with delight,
Nor moving to the left or the right,
Through star-tripped.

The marriage bed,
The unborn moment, hung.
The thin bone of the dead
Then clasped the head
Where innocence had sung.

AN EPITHALAMIUM

OR

MARRIAGE DAY IN A LITTLE-KNOWN COUNTRY

A MARRIAGE POEM FOR AN AGE

THE YOUNG WOMEN

WE have loved the self, each other, and the rounded slope,
For being young abrupt shapes with abrupt words hurt.
Finding that we could not know ourselves, we turned to catch
our reflection,
And meeting our difference, we felt less apart.
Where the shallow hills are curved, the grain may run iron
ore,
And every heartless height holds some slight green.
Daughters of rock-climbers, fumbling in dark valleys,
Naturally drawing from our history the sure step, and the
lean
Unpampered war cry, or instructor of immediate action,
Yet we choose an airy present of not giving, hugging the slope
against the shale.
Now our virginity has gone, with the first step,
And our minds—allowing growth—have already dreamt the
male and the female.
These are no longer boys that we see, but men. We are no
longer girls but women.

THE YOUNG MEN

Now we shall listen to the tall grass and the trees.
More beautiful than our morning song that clapped back
from the peak
Are the things that breathe about us on this day.
We put down our hands and kneel upon the ground to hear
it speak,

Returning an unpremeditated dream in glad reply.
What is the time, the hour? On the hill we see a child pluck-
ing flowers:
The round face of the day is seeded with infinities.
In our minds the children stamp, the strict parent frowns,
the infant cowers
Behind random clusters, the flower-symbol, to smother laugh-
ter.
Compact and kneeling, we smoothe the wet grass to one side,
Learning to touch the earth with consideration,
Knowing that we must be less militant and young to stroke
the things that hide.
Even the bright dew weeps from the stem at our inept and
thoughtless touch.

THE YOUNG WOMEN

Fear with us was care. Nature had commended us to life,
And flocking, smiling, nodding, we hid our exactions closed
beneath lids.
Some of us paused, some gambled and unflowered at the brink;
Most of us knew cathedral choirs and envisioned noisy steeples
in our heads;
But now all the images of earth have soared and bedded down
in space.
Care is the mother of the moment whose arms we drop.
Thrusting aside blossoms from the face, we open our eyes and
stare.
Released from our guard, we see the night birds swoop
Across unlidded pools down to the hollowed valleys.
The day is here! Run, and lift the small child with its flower.
The little ones have been gathering since the first streak.
Old mouths, calling the new dawn with remembered clatter,
Have not left unblessed our history, the crevice or the crags.

Let us speak long together of this wooing and our thought.
Beside the water, each of us must strip and take direction,
Knowing that we must move within a destined pattern.
Bending our steps alone from the bank to the liquid desolation,
We perceive that an act of life will fling us through the void,
The spirit of possession, whirling us, with insensate sound
That thins at last, and pointing out, ejects us into quiet.
Marvelous are those stars that hold, and those waters that wind,
The inert mountains, lashed down by the pines and streams.
No lover, considering the day of his marriage, should envy the hawk its height!
We anticipate many whispers
In which death extends to life some portion in the brood-world of the night.
It is not only the female fact that we meet here: it is the river into sea and the bared peninsula.

THE YOUNG WOMEN

Dance while we are young. (There is an old dance of the mind.)
Articulate all the movements that are mute in step.
The deep mouth of the wind sucks in its breath.
Our skirts are so high in blowing, a little wild are the notes that keep
The time, that sing out of the past the tune of the deleted swan.
Our betrothed come to us over the flower-rabble of the hill,
Glad that we learned to smile, for laughter would have tired us,
And tears appeared to be denial of the will.
We took all the variations of the self and pressed about the one

Until every particle of fact was faced and we were no longer
  wine-sick on love,
Nor laughter-ridden, nor tear-dazed, but strangely open,
As conscious innocents who understand and do not reprove.
O wind, put down our skirts! Let us fold our hands, be firm
  and neat.
The Puritan, poised in brief reminder, cracks the placid pond,
And we would not remind the correct back or the tight beak
  of our wedding night.
If some of us have stretched upon dark grass for other hearts
  to tend,
More have turned up pebbles or shouted down the channels
  of wells.

THE YOUNG MEN

We mount the irregular land and halt the advance,
As people expanding into dreamt-of but unmapped country.
Only by the celt and the sign, the earthwork and the roads,
Shall we be able to give form to the early inhabitants, the free
Intrepid man. You have said that yours was the heritage of
  rock-climbers.
Together we shall give the seed and the fruit that grows
  explicit in its step.
Rejecting no light or shade, leaping from crag to slope in the
  sun,
Drumming with the heels on the earth, the head on the rim
  of the day, till the inanimates weep,
And generations hold their pain with knowledge of impend-
  ing laughter,
The wide becomes unfathomable, and the parent, stiff with
  history,
Exhorts the spirit of the future in the child.
Room for the irrelevant allows our act of love its mystery
In which the cult of nights abound and images of life take
  on the attitudes of sleep.

Look into our eyes, for there is nothing there unknown.
At every turn we see some black direction that grows grave
with light.
We pity those who lift back the morning and sink into barren
dark,
Where there is no deviation from a lasting end in sight.
Here is the harvest, the hand extending, a floor to the sea and
the air above.
We are not waters to be drowned in, nor have we submerged
rocks for wrecking.
Where storms are, you have met our temper; the crackle of
high leaves our talk.
Our love is a whip to the winter wind, and our sleep the corn
clinging
Over the full round acres of inhabited land.
What wisdom can we bring you that we have not found to-
gether?
Each morning we wake up out of the same mother place,
With the same animal blinking as the lizard, paused and
neuter,
Before discovering ourselves and then our shape.
Our life is a nakedness moving through tormented weather
with a will.
Living with man, we cannot be apart from any fraction of
the kind.
Come, O come to us, so that we shall know more of the pine
against the hill.
Lovers may touch, but the marriage bond is a link without
distraction.

BOOK FOUR

THERE IS A ROCKY JUT, FLUNG LIKE A DISC

THERE is a rocky jut, flung like a disc
      Against the dull dim roll of sea and sky.
I have heard, I have heard of the place,
And now I see it from the walls of a city
Choked with rubble and the thoughtless
Droppings of the curlews nesting the brood,
And playing their wings with the whim of the wind
In the streams and rills of the air.

The sea is a slate, impenetrable as steel
That the birds dent and rebound from
With listless monotony of movement.
As I gaze from the cracked and broken pane
Of an old stained window of the desolate church,
My eyes reaching the light
Between the dull flutter of thought that rebounds
Like the cry and the proud rush of wings,
I am stirred to a strange compassion.

Bells, bells, bells, bells of a steeple ringing!
Wind in the bell-loft ringing!

The walls and the streets of the town
In grey ruins tumbling deep to the surface of the sea
Rest at last in the silver orb of the sun.

Now the deep wine and emerald, vermilion and gold,
An illusion of dream veils the symbol of the symbol,
Puts its seal upon the head, a birthmark to the bone.

Down from the window where they stood in time,
Balanced in man's brief moment for them,

Three apostles, nameless as the thought of them.
Oh, speak to me not of their benignity,
Of the hair that fell, a dusty mist of vivid foam,
Or the wonder of their own eternity!
With arms flung up to roll the world, a pebble
On the palm, the wine-red and the emerald, purple and
    gold . . .

There is a rocky jut, flung like a disc against
The dull dim roll of sky,
And here, like sad pilgrims, left godless in a moment,
They stood, their hands caught at the neck,
Poised in the fold of each own thought,
Each hand the delicate incantation to a timeless span.
He in wine held with the fingers ever at the throat,
He in emerald able to point toward the far horizon;
He in the purple and the gold will bear the star.

But what of the form that stirs across the edge,
Wind whipping up the skirt about the legs?

TIME WAS LIKE THE SNAIL

TIME was like the snail in his cupolaed house.
   He admitted the shutters up in the day but down at
   night.
Time was the snail in his cupolaed house.

In the evening, when the birds gathered in branches,
The long evening dusk, and the hills' slender haunches
Reclining, and stretching to the edge—
Now in the evening, armed up, and gathered to the ledge,
Precipitating toward the lake to shallow-foot the water,
Strode down the proud man's daughter.

Eager eyes eyeing the leaning sky,
The one unbranched bird giving its unplaced cry,
The turbulent titter of disturbed fish sounding water,
Neither disturbed nor stopped the proud man's daughter.
The rocks and the slim fish of quick river walked beside the
      child;
This girl, the woman and the rock were neither meek nor
      mild.

Slowly the fox curved out its robin plume
And poising, lashed out its shrill yap to the moon,
Clipping the crouched grouse from the brush,
Twisting to catch it on its upward rush.
And still the lake remained immune to sound,
And stiffly the girl looked down and not around.

In the evening, men may come to water,
And men may cool their hands in water,
And stare upon the daughter,
The proud man's bathing daughter;
Round is the slope and round the tired man's daughter.

I am singing as a lover.
The birds are perched.
O, my love, how may I tell you
That one star has slipped to your hand?
O, my love, how few tears
Do you know? How many you demand.
I am singing as a lover.

Again I am singing as a lover.
I know that the water covers you from me.
May I know that my plucking will tell something?
I have left the land and have come to this place.
O, my love, how few tears!
Do you know that I should live without home or race?
I am singing as a lover.

A CHILD'S MEDITATION AND PRAYER
AFTER NOT DYING

THERE is simple promise to be put forward.
  Let it be as God leaning down to my hand;
Let it be as a pact with men and women;
Let it be with the child that I would bear of mind and womb,
And the lover with his sadness and his wonder,
With his troubled heart that finds small rest,
Who sees his own time in his own way,
Never easily putting upon himself its shabbiness.

I talked of some light, caught from some vast mental jungle,
Whirled like an idiot top, and woke to find myself quite beast,
The gibbering monkey . . . this in a dream of optical opaque-
      ness.
Always the head, always the head and jungle, one vast jungle,
Spinning, spinning, spinning, spun,
Dignity, morality, humanity, the sun,
Cleanliness, directness, and eternal wanting of the truth,
The glint of abstruse truth.

What time is there for spinning worn-out thread,
Seeing ape ancestry, knowing the gutter that would be
If one foot were placed one half-breadth over.

As the gravity of sky, untouched and mute in peace,
Stares with its supreme unity into my eyes,
Knowing me hardly the fittest to survive,
Yet, having gazed so, while some prodding man
Saved me for another day's living
When my child life had swung on one mere hair of existence,
It would unconsciously shrug and say the will must live,
Even now when the adult longs and droops to have its claims.

What is it that I must swear to men, who have been slightly
    gentle,
What must I swear to these men, who have been gentle in their
    way,
Who have given, knowing or unknowing, few but structural
    shapes?
What do I offer to the earliest years and my homeland,
The force that swept me from my land to be saved from dying?

This is the hour that means the end of trying to break
The paralyzing power of mind,
Knowing so simply as I do the pattern of my days,
The good exercise of emotional abstemiousness,
On the one hand abstinence, on the other will,
The hour to be as one among people, as head above animal,
As quiet among noise, as heart among stone,
As intrepid courage among wastrel fear.

The hand moves now and there lies the cracked and crying
    pact,
The many times annihilate pact.

Father, not of pity, not of sweetness,
But as one who moves and yet remains still,
Who knows neither unliving nor life,
Who meets all objects, knows the shape and yet is edgeless in
    the self,
What you have given me is good in my eyes,
What you have spread shall become as something good forever
    in my eyes.

THERE WAS A DEVIL THAT SLIPPED

THERE was a devil that slipped.
   Immaculate wings carried him in.
(He had bought them the day before.)
Pretty little goblin, with bright new wings,
And such a sense of humor!
Now? he thought. Where? he thought.
Just then I stood.
I happened to be little too just then.
I had my own thoughts and not much more.
And he knew things rather well.
He carried a good show of sins
In Christmas packages,
Paper, all covered with gold stars
That stuck on badly and kept coming off
In the wind.
Well, he saw me and smiled.
Here's luck! Get them as young as you can.
That made me smile too,
Though I had my thoughts
And not much time for more.
Here's a package for you, youngster!
He cried cheerily.
A package of stars?
Hell, no! They're only on the outside,
He said.
A fine present to keep you busy in the head
Ad infinitum; that's what it is.
We both laughed at that.
And then he shot off to find some more devilment.
I was a bit too easy.
A package of stars! he snorted.
Good Lord! There's more uncertainty,
Inaction and incompleteness

In one sniff of that starry little article
Than there are stars in the blue up there,
Or mischief in the whole tilt of my head.

BOOK FIVE

THE ANCHORITE

(THE HERMIT SEES THROUGH A MONTH'S DREAMING.)

I CAME up to a house on the mountain
  And sat in a room, smoking and talking to myself:
(There is one devil that goes up in the blue strand.)
"It is the division that makes me find pain
To hurt myself with, to die upon, to laugh at myself;
It is the terrible face of the wrinkled land."

"Fifty years have gone by on every side, I know.
A body tires and dries up and a stamp is made between the eyes.
To come upon a tremble of spring here upon the mountain . . .
It is as if an ancient bone gave a low
Girl's laugh, and I must hold the ugliness stiff for the torment
     and the sighs.
A witch is more lovely than thought in the mountain rain."

I came up to the house with its winter hemlock;
The sun drilled down into my delight, and I spoke:
"I have not loved a woman with beautiful feet;
I have stroked myself and leapt but have not found the witches'
     wedlock,
Over the hill I thrust the long strand of smoke.
Here is myself to laugh with and the high cock's self-defeat."

THERE HAS BEEN MORE THAN
BEGINNING AND END TO FACE

THERE has been more than beginning and end to face,
     More than thirst and eventual storm and famine:
There is the strange disharmony of mind and spirit
(Gift of time, family and uncertain heritage)
Oh, and the unhealth of wrong thought and fear!—
The dullness, arch naïveté and infanthood!
For here lies sin against the simplest law,
Leisure, satanic slough, and rude despond
(The image-worship building in the so-called abstract mind,
Where channels made never may unscar themselves).
Death acts: freak masks the crimes against symmetrical law.

What I have not done, but seeded in my thought,
Felt quivering into half-life through my frame
(And so attempted to drown in shout and noise,
In loud primitive ejaculation, and brute moving
Against the logic and sweetness of my proper brain)
Are unforgivable, in the ways of balancing;
In the truth, that we surmise—unquestioning—to be human;
In the beauty, that is inherent in our meaning:
These are the deeds that have broken tablets and disinherited!

Come, let me grasp the power and the basic law!
Let me know the hand that is of a peculiar coolness!
I give the simple promise of self-will, of abstinence, all that is
     conquering:
That mind be grave and life be adequate.

I WOULD HOLD THE MANY SIDES
OF LOVE WITH MY TWO HANDS

I WOULD hold the many sides of love with my two hands,
  Knowing, in the hot-cool and overt curve,
That once caught from mind: the inflexible demands
Of time, death attendant upon life, all life to serve,
Foetus, light-engendered.

When seeing angular children running over bright grass,
Follow the pace, the action and direct child's glance,
Each umbered, innocent and shrilling as they pass.
The shock of sound, the race and stare mark, in the erratic ad-
    vance
Across sub-smooth, neither song nor bleak but vital fact.

The brain, a moon of mother-calm and fertile,
Unfertile in the ultimate of meticulous placement,
Every man, having figured, having tested, attempts to widen
    to non-sterile.
Only the gentle-tempered mind conceives of its development
In sweet proportion and as such propitious.

It is here and now, the love, the running child, the mind,
Recall divergent sides and selves, that walk,
Move as a pattern under God, expose to the natural loom the
    web of kind.
Love, the child, the thought, and to the crest, the metaphysic
    hawk,
Finite conscience, star-based in the vaster unspecific.

How would he break and how suspend, when dead
In the passionate drowning, the climactic action of our living,
The fears that hold in the tight seed, the covetous bed?

89

How supersede the intolerant tense for the more than giving,
The tolerant circle that transcends its shape?

To hold the many sides of love with my two hands,
Neither too condescending the touch nor bitter-brim the hour,
But draw from amphibious tides the underlying concept of
    quiet sands.
Water! Land! Each gull and hawk the height of cerebral
    power.
Recede from the body somewhat. Extend the fragile precepts
    of hieratic soul.

MEN AND WOMEN HAVE MEANING
ONLY AS MAN AND WOMAN

MEN and women have meaning only as man and woman.
The moon is itself and it is lost among stars.
The days are individual, and in the passage
The nights are each sleep, but the dreams vary.
A repeated action is upon its own feet.
We who have spoken there speak here.
A world turns and walks away.
The timing of independent objects
Permits them to live and move and admit their space
And entity and various attitudes of life.
All things are cool in themselves and complete.

BELIEVE ME, MY FEARS ARE ANCIENT

BELIEVE me, my fears are ancient,
   And I deal in ancient patterns.
Like the burst into spring, I am defiant
As the shoot, while the bare earth turns;

As the gull from the unpecked shell
Recalls the one act of living,
Totters and breaks pell-mell
With the stark demand for winging;

As the embryo dream moves from the void
Together with the will to be,
Out of the welter and span, denuded,
Into the spawning sea.

In the clear sway of movement,
The contact at various corners,
The mind in the head has content
In spite of conglomerate mourners,

And rejoices to slip over and be convivial;
Yet always there stride strange shapes,
And the gibbers of unenviable
Fears swing like promiscuous apes.

Believe me, I am lapped by fears,
Split and contaminated:
A jungle life out of the jungle peers,
Though the sun gleams unabated.

HERE WHERE I TAMPER WITH THE INVERTED WALLS OF TOMORROW

HERE where I tamper with the inverted walls of tomor-
  row,
The gathering of old women about their bagpipe sorrow
In the dry room of their choice,
On each knee a cup (erotic age!), virginity in every voice,
The strident, tired and cryptic knitting
Clattering on and on, while my fingers, flitting
Over impregnable surface warm with the friction,
Callous, ice-smooth with the next day's obscurity of action . . .
Here where I finger, only yesterday having thudded out
With an evil beat, that leapt from extremities of doubt
Till even the head threshed, the pauper skull
Acclaimed itself in every drum the Caliban of dull,
The height of down, the unnumbered telephone operator,
The stammering apologetic political debater,
With blowing papers on an evening pier,
Once having dreamt the speech and equipoise subordinately
  dear.

Leave the head to its particular swimming,
The hand as fist where it belongs, the finger to its skimming.
Know the new, and meet again the adult,
Walk the path with men and women, and consult
The attitudes of little children,
Treat with gravity the statements of the parrot and the hen,
Run with your hands in pockets, whistling, and listen to sharp
  wisdom
From your own spontaneous play, even from
The clip of your heels under night lamps and on in the dark,
While hieroglyph trees are marked thin and bare about the
  winter park.

These are the tools of questioning to be met and used every-
    where,
To be bumped into, like workmen with thin collars high in the
    morning air:
Such people, mistaken by the careless for the unancestored,
Born of reflex, the machine, with its virginity of assembled
Parts, non-life, to live birth, death and food,
Without choice to feel the devil or the good.

Time who pours, the terrible mother of fruition,
A brisk director of pageantry, war and balanced inclination,
Narrow in sense, repetitive in ideology and plan,
Endlessly creative in detail, spares each man
The head to dream, the brief right to turn and lift his hand,
To shout some hate, some gladness and some pain to some de-
    mand.

About the hill and valley striding, small the moment, Godhead
Works the rhythm of the race over the race's silenced dead,
Who have gathered time with all the little perceptions abbrevi-
    ated,
Shading their eyes, and breathing jerkily in uneven rows of the
    belated,
Each calm clarity hanging its head to forgetfulness,
For each drooped man and shame and each too cruel distress.

Panting is over, the hand loosed from the hair,
The long tempered point implies a touch from wall to air,
The surface fingering of the inexplicable desire
Of the infant, who has been pulled one step, but being young,
    must wait to ascend the next step higher.

POEM INTO SLEEP

IN the night we peopled evil forests,
 Running naked with our hands against our mouths,
Leaping from the channels to the brief hill-crests,
Frantic at the panting bog and the cypress wreaths.

Now in this sleep we river-run,
Eye to eye, mouth to mouth unspoken;
For rock is flesh and the oval sun
Eye to eye, mouth to mouth unspoken.

Walls of early smoke the leaves,
Each in an autumn's roisterous trail.
Even the dream a pulse of sheaves
Out of the hoar-mist tangled and frail.

Scale of the lifting eye on-set;
Oh, and a sigh and the pass of years.
The red-bent sea-spliced season met
Only to flay our primordial fears.

A NIGHT SPENT IN WATCHING

A NIGHT spent in watching
A night spent in watching
Night.
A half-wing of thought lifted
And drifted
Out.
Thought in answer to awareness
Of thought in awareness
Of night.

She is the sphinx with stretched eyes,
And the coiled blue of her hair flies
At the moon.
The weight of her lips pressed and pressed
On the heads of the blessed
Half-dead,
She speaks, and her words are the mumblings
Of the infinite to the jumblings
Of the dead.
She is a deep-bosomed she-cat watching
The sun with green eyes watching
The night.

The dark trees shiver at the paleness
Of the dead-awake, pressed in frailness
Out,
And they grow hushed within themselves
As the dead-awake wander within themselves
Out.

She is the sphinx with stretched eyes,
Stretched green at the corners, and she lies
In desolation.

INSTINCT AND SLEEP

INSTINCT and sleep, you are two passages that converge—
 Two faces that stare and reflect back one vision.
The sea and the night both stir their profound surge,
Each shouldering on the boundary of their prison.
A man who has raised the inhibited line of far-off horizon
Will stretch his thought to the beach where the two converge.

Now—as the man starts up to follow out the shape
That the welding of a dream and touching of a present
Has clipped out and moulded of horizon and the cape,

Dunes, whose cool sands wash up and meet the sea,
And all the slopes aslant, and thin-lipped blue
Waves, with their fists and their shapes drubbing,
Evolving dry bubbles at their thin-lipped spitting,
Immaculated waves, wind-flipping—

Run I down to the water; and sea, run up to me!
I am rolled in your uneven turbulence and mind,
I'm adulted in your poised pant and pawing;
And lightly gulls and birds are cawing.
I am bent to the coast line running.

SLEEP, WHOSE HOUR HAS COME

SLEEP, whose hour has come,
  With fine fingers and lean lid,
The end and sum
Of the day passed through!

Sleep, who walks by the water,
And knows the deep
Rather as the woman, quizzical, her
Mind placed for the leap
That is inevitable at dark!

Beds may be banks.
Seas may be happier beds.
Soldiers that drowse in ranks
With cool earth under their heads
Drowse with a timelessness.

Sleep the sum and end of a day!
Calmly the pattern of our instinct
Patters its inconsistent say,
And sleep is still retribute.

RIVER OF LIGHT

RIVER of light
Bombard the night,
Or what have we to say?
This is a little thing?
Or, shall we sing?

We had built this, seed on seed, two grains for every thousand
    years.
You must not forget us, now we bear other seeds.
In long deep rivers of Lethe, you may not forget us,
Or those you would forget, and yet must build upon.
· All the immutable stone and great earth,
All the days that are to night what this is to man
And the shouldering hills through musky hollowed dawns
Precipitate the shadowing sidling flanks of the past
And future.
We had ancestors, high mighty men, with beards that flipped
    in the wind,
A little wind; for there were gales to see in the pregnant stare
    that they turned along the land.
It is earth, they cried, earth! And the rains came down,
And the far plowed fields burst up with a new clean bell of
    green,
A very sound, rung in the temper of the newborn spring.
I think that the old men must have turned upon the stars
And whispered in a young world's ear,
Shoving the cracked palms of their hands against the ground,
    while their fine
White heads caught and held and dropped with each return
Of sun, each wisc thought and half-formed dream.

Those are thoughts without words that make him sing.
Those are the hands that cup rust like the tail of a fox,

The bodies of half-dead, half-dreamed wavering along the line,
Making faint patterns in the caked clay of their brittle bones,
Small, incredible as they grow into the stone we build upon.

Now we turn to you, great cities, and we are dumb with our
     own doing.
These were spun of our heads, and whether they will be the
     tombs and testaments of tomorrow,
Whether they will look with great incorruptible eyes into the
     tomorrow,
And bear us witness to a better race, we do not know.

Do we mock ourselves with turrets, mosques and cupolas brittle,
Light spattering out the gilt and feathers of a brash pale people?
Is this a world that sings its own song and ends within it?

Or is it at last the flutter and cry of an eagle startled up?
Of all the eyes that drub along the surface, will there be one to
     catch beyond the moment?
High as the dark that trudges into night, the cities beat,
The incalculable pouring of mass streams into the streets
Of the meeting of man and woman,
Like cool stone poured to the palm of a corrupt shivering
Back to tangle and be lost—the strand of water weed.

The old men whispered stars, and this is a new world.
We were blown a great insoluble riddle by some triton horn,
Out of the corridor, the twist and curl of soundless seas.
An aboriginal tribe of fingering sun-bewildered life
Out of the deep dusk spiraling, beyond the enigmatic spleen,
Only to return, only to return through the pale wash of the
     shallow,
Like shoals of minnows spawning down to the tides.
It is for the young to dream their dreams if they have heads,

And the old and the wise to see what they must see.
These are tremendous steps, imponderable strides,
But infinitely small, like notes of a piping across the painted
  hills.

I FEEL ONLY THE DESOLATION
OF WIDE WATER

I FEEL only the desolation of wide water,
Its back a silver dimpling from the sun.
I feel only the thrill, the far cry of one gull
Reluctantly chasing its shadow on the wave.
Here, like some lost strand of seaweed,
I remain within myself a sad contumely.

Mark, mark the ring of bells, the tap of wings!
Mark, mark, my eyes that turn a sad pool up;
For I remember how the yellow sand slipped
Through my fingers and the night drew a tight
Cloak warmly about my yellow sand-stained skin.

Oh, to what shame toward my own first cause,
I find that like both sea and air I am two things:
Crystal and clear and on the other hand sweet mad.

There is a boat with perpendicular sails,
White as the heart of the wind.
I would ask where you blew, you boat with sail,
If I did not know that the seams of you were cracked.

How the gulls cover the water, the path to the sun.
How their wings drift and lift them up.
They move as simply as the rise and fall of waves.
And I would move as simply as the rise and fall of waves.

EVEN THE GULLS OF THE COOL ATLANTIC

THE gulls of the cool Atlantic tip the foam.
The boats that warn me of fog warn me of their motion.
I have looked for my childhood among pebbles, and my home
Within the lean cupboards of Mother Hubbard and neat Al-
bion.

A wind whose freshness blows over the cape to me
Has made me laugh at the thought of a friend whose hair is
blond.
Still I laugh and place my hands across the sea
From the farthest stretch of lands to the end of the end.

I had so often run down to these shores to stare out.
If I took an island for a lover and Atlantic for my sheet,
There was no one to tell me that loving across distance would
turn about
And make the here and now an elsewhere of defeat.

In my twenty-first year to have the grubby hand and slums,
Be the small child at my knee, my knee the glistening chalk
That sails to meet the stationary boat, the water sloping as it
comes,
And all the Devon coast of grey and abrupt rock.

By gazing across water I have flicked many gulls from my eyes,
Shuffled small shells and green crabs to my feet.
The day is cool; the sun bright; the piper cries
Shrilly, tempering the untouched sand in delicate retreat.

Up beyond the height and over the bank, I have a friend.
How is your winter night and summer action?

There need be little more than a teacup hour to make us both comprehend
A mature man's simplicity or grave child's sweet reaction.

WHERE THERE ARE WINGS CONTRITE

WHERE there are wings contrite,
    White fronds, quivering out
Without time or space
To limit the weightless lift and bend,
Air and the sea, bubble-hollowed
To hold a silver wind
Only existent to the white cup
Of innumerable dipped wings;
Here let us wander a moment,
That tears may fall in silence
As the sea-spray flies
And dribbles back to sea.

Here let us wander aimlessly,
Remembering also that one tear,
Welled down eternity,
Dripped beyond worlds
To make this infinite sea.
And yet must we echo
That large happiness with little sighs?

Come, touch the hand of my loneliness,
Slender as fluted wings against the sky,
As the evening wind is the breath
Of some more hidden shade
Absently poised between air and air,
The shallows and the void.

OF PLAINS OF SAND THAT SPEND THEMSELVES

OF plains of sand that spend themselves cherished by the early moon,
Of minute moments in a breath of wind drawn deep to the lungs,
Of that there is none, of home, of that there is none
To stretch to in all madcap inadequacy,
Of many things existent and nonexistent, cupped to the hollow meaning.
In this I have the philosophy of irrelevance.
And yet a fiddlestring bowed on and on can only ache with that bleak fingering.
When I pause, what is there to say in words?
I can then see only tepidity, O river!
Mother, mother! My heart is like twin infants suckling dew out of grass
When there should be roisterous breasts,
When there should be cornstalks whacking their vivid sweep
Into the core that barren bears tombs, tombs, more tombs.
Mother, you have born the inevitable twins, of bald conception;
Therefore I do not cry more militant in words.
I merely say my say, as, when the day is grey,
Of simpering tirades in young girls,
Of tireless quality of innuendo in the shades,
Of things incalculable, unquestionable, abstruse,
Leapt out of the irresolute self that lies in me
Cool, cool, and, oh, let there be stars for this irresolute flute.

IT IS NOT I WHO AM SLEEPING
IN THE ROCK

IT is not I who am sleeping in the rock under the wood,
  Nor are my limbs congested with cities or the leaves:
I am lifting and dropping night and day with a good grace,
Each after each in their immoderate halves.

I have no memory to inflict unless I may sing to you,
And the weight covering my mouth holds me back.
The valleys will repeat my secret in a few
Wordless blares, or the hunter track

Toward the hollow of the brain that I would not admit
(Being the place of fawns in the angles of the tree,
The child's bound corner, or the limit
The birds must instinctively secrete in flight, or be

Swept into the erotic sun, or the edgeless tide beneath).
It is not I who am sleeping in the rock or the wedge,
And yet I thrust back the wrinkled earth for breath,
And in the dark extend thin wind-stalked fingers to extract
The brittle ledge.

BOOK SIX

THE COMING OF STRANGE PEOPLE

(Written on the day of Holland's invasion)

SO many bodies flat upon the stir of spring.
   We know too well the old war chanting,
The intense green fields that have arms
And all that is the day of man in fallow.
Bitter I am at the sky for its coolness,
My head against the earth, and this my earth.

Strange people, where are you stepping?
"Men we are, with our beautiful evils pointed.
How lovely are our demons, how silver winged—
The shout of their droppings in our throats."
Is it hate you have for the world then?
Strange people, would you have less of us?

It is a bewildered age that talks back and forth,
One man's eye to the ground, another to the space.
From this land we see the valleys and the banners.
The hollow places will hold ruins for a time;
Then the sides of the mountain will green and flower,
Even women shall bear trees and know the leaves for children.

My city, what an ugliness I have given you!
Earth, there is no gentle shaping of the clay.
Time, no building in the hour.
Things come and the sea is sea without us.
All is brash and shrill, with bone to fallow on,
And bitter of mouth are we who taste the green this spring.

THE SPEED OF PLANES WAS STILL UPON THE NOON

THE speed of planes was still upon the noon;
The whirling planet stuttered and drew up.
Reaction in all quiet corners tongued its inactivity;
Windows were slammed and men stood circles of eternity.

Words once spoken spoke themselves.
Trees lavished the hour with leaves muttering,
And arms extending scissor-clipped the wind.
Rocks blocked their way, allowed the atom to titter and be
    kind.

Each misplaced was replaced again;
If tumbling was not known, tumbling was admitted;
And you were there, alive, awake in your dead places,
A well patient among similar well cases.

AHAB THE SUPERMONOMANIAC

AN IMPROVISATION

AHAB, the supermonomaniac . . .
        The finite creation leaguing it
Through the torturous underseas of un-God . . .
Sought all life damned.
Pain chanted imaginings.

Ahab, the strain of the inexplicable,
The man-fathomed bitterness.
We who turn slowly,
Forcing our consciousness to conceive of passivity
In land, in night, in stone . . .
We, who are rocked to the bottom by our own inability
To dent, to stammer, or to guide, to restrain
The slow annihilation of the coast,
The shift, the imperceptible movement of inanimate
Dissolving all along the line . . .

ON LOOKING AT LEFT FIELDS

IN the old fields the old corn tangles.
   Remember, these lands were green;
See how the sleek weed twists and strangles.
There is more here than is seen.

Dried leaves like lizard scales over the land
And the slow blink down to winter.
Father of shivering times, crazed by each spring's demand,
Why would you know your daughter?

It is this London they will never know—
Something of must, stale bread and spring,
The fattened dog, the thinning child and Rotten Row.
To be born a Londoner, as I, gives meaning to the thing.

LONDON

LONDON sits with her hands cupped.
   The day has been quiet in spring.
Only street calls and the far burrs of traffic disrupt
The gentle sun, the sleek grey string
Of pigeons wedged on building tops.
A few cock sparrows stuff the crop with dung,
Following a fat-flanked mare as she clops,
Flipping out her lips where the nose bag hung.

London sits with her hands cupped.
The pigeons scatter, pink etched feet
Leaving no mark on the shelved, erupt
And timeworn weathered street.
Up and down, the doors shine, newly painted,
Here a cherry red among the greys and browns,
The brass polished and the steps a sainted
Smoothness of well-scrubbed white.

All the flat fronts gaze immobile. Windows blink.
Doors press their frames in rows of chaste warm color,
While slim weeds of ivy slink
With a gayer sheen against the duller.

London sits with her hands bent,
Letting a later light spill into golden pools.
Easter lilies carried home speak of an early Lent,
Winding the quieter thought on the quieter spools.
All the spring is flagging its way with lily and daffodil
Till a cool breeze speaks out of some darker street,
Clouds shuffle up with restless intrepidity, and spill
Their whole river of abundance at her feet,
The whole clean wide river, and wrap her in one river of sleet,
Her sides in one wet sheet.

EMPIRE NOW DEAD AND MAYFLOWER

LFRACOMB is a sea-town where rocks elbow
  The head of the island-once-kingdom . . .
Beaches slightly sanded and low,
Promontories denying the weight of water,
Here and there gull-splattered, weed-colored, some
Stained to an even brittle green and sheen like handled pewter:

An old shape, where thought has not forgotten
The seeming town, here going up the hills,
And there down to the bottom, errant men,
These several people passing by vined gates
And high slabbed walls. The smell that fills
Salt odor with something more than salt invigorates.

Then know what it is to have the sins of the father!
To have had childhood here by water
And not to have had wide eyes to gather,
Eyes nor mind, to undry the stalk that sucked time dry,
Not to have opened bright blood to the body earth, and there
Fed lust for good with good, relived the primordial cry.

Sea and articulate brain of Devon Rock
Jutting fine bones of England down the coast!
Years off the sea and the joints of the city mock
At what we have gained, and shriveled, from out of the age.
Green and the forest, lost with the ancient host,
Voice in bleak water torn a last god's fearful rage.

Mayflower, with so many angling their eyes
Away from the early home toward the Cape,
Wild in their look, their mouths wet with the sea and bitter
  sighs,
From converging sources flapping irresolute sail,

Nowhere they turn today can they escape:
Wherever they touch, the land draws thin and frail.

    A sailor balanced on a spar!
    And even the gull will wind you far,
    Even the slow heave of the whale,
    Lifting the gunwale with its tail!
    O my love, what sea has bound you?
    What evening passage along the shore?
    O my love, what sea has found you
    On the salt night's deep sea floor?

    A sailor balanced on a spar,
    Blue-eyed, squat, an English tar,
    O my love, forever lost,
    The boat and spar forever tossed,
    An English tar . . .

An Englishman, and down to the leaving boat . . .
We were Empire and now we are dead or Mayflower,
Our faces old ballads shaping themselves afloat,
So many bubbles, with fish, with wanness, with sleep.
Ilfracomb is a child's village, a hill once tower.
Wave once alive against Devon coast and a child's inordinate
    leap.

I am these shores. I am my past, the village and the hill,
Wherever sea comes with its distance opened
Out to the end and edge to precipitate the will.
The Cape, the fishing village, the dunes! Only the water comes,
Only that, to be with, to run into, and to be drowned,
To be buried, breast of what has been running to sea.

Again I saw in the clear icy spring
Lives I had lived and many people before me.

Nothing of man or God had relieved the sting
Of departure from other coasts and cliffs,
Rigging strung like a bow arrowed irresolutely,
We with the bone-dry throats flung in the strange man's skiffs

Only to be what one was, one is, and one becomes.

SPEAKING TO EXILES—THE ONE EXILE

SPEAKING to Exiles, the one Exile:
   Memory, two wedged women
(Sparse hair, New England boned),
Will know you in your bed,
Will find you as you lie wan-faced,
Staring toward sand, into sea, and dead.

Count your joints! Gather yourself!
You said aloneness was the flute.
Take upon your knee each meaning,
See what your infants are.
Now you will shiver alone—alone!
Water is thin spread far.

Exile the sprung bow turned into splint.
Yet does that make bewilderment the more?
The equivalent of God is now to find him.
It is the return of epic man;
It is the ring of legend dissected;
It is the clock where sands once ran.

On my knees are two hands.
Those hands, these knees, are mine.
Under the sun, I am articulate
Laughter, and still by the edge of my brother.
In what modern ship-thing did I sail?
Unwomb me now, my mother!

Speaking to Exiles, the one Exile:
Words are yours, and knowing—
In profile smoking blue smoke
At tables or in far rooms,
Grasping to hold this book, that line—
Whether the frantic age declines or looms,

Islands are mothers into sea,
Sons the frail gulls circling—
Circling without minds or lives,
Balanced in wind, unborn, undone.
Now, wrung at the breaking, there are tears:
Exile, you are unmothered; the islands are gone.

AND THOUGH IT IS EVENING
AND I AM TIRED

AND though it is evening and I am tired,
I watch the lean meticulous architect's hand
Gather and space the all too harsh demand;

As spider with slender entwined knees,
Spun clockwise by avalanched honeybees,
Turns to the subtle weaving of a more insidious web.

So much of laughter in the head,
So much of the golden apple and the racing,
The craft-won game and tricks of placing.

Now the garden and the mental laughter still,
Rejection never given, never made, stands freak upon the hill.
Laughter is better quiet: the smile is heard.

Images of spare Madonnas, Mary Magdalene and Christ,
The uneven walk and garrulous seeking wine-bowl;
All loud reflection on the somewhat soul.

Bend the head to the outcupped hand.
This is the age for shabby forms and contraband.
Life's macabre and every night's replete with its defeats.

We are allowed to place one foot before the other,
To know some valley or some slaty sea,
To hear with weary calm that being born to live, we must live
    to be.

There is small love lost in this strained hour.
Youth dropped down has only dreamt the flower.

The dance of death now cries out for the undivulged tomorrow.

And though it is evening and I am tired,
I will gather myself to the mountains
And chant out my voice to that primal unsexed quiet till
doomsday for my pains.

THERE IS A BURSTING OF THE PULSE OF TIME

THERE is a bursting of the pulse of time
   That, like some giant thing, seems born anew,
And also, like the swift passing of the weighted lime
Bears on a tune, that infinity drew
Again and yet again from her seared pouch . . .
And built the puny arms of day
Across the feeble rollings of a restless couch.

One might dream that by lifting the hand to flay
The wanderings of a passing cloud
There would be rebuilt again the whispered dreams
Of man—strong golden hands, straight back, godlike, proud—
Sweeping the wind through bones and streams
Of his own dry salt sweat and blood.

But no, this bursting of the pulse of time
Is nothing but the leaking of green mud
Eating its way through this grinning pantomime—
To bear the fruit that holds an odor of a future
Carried inch by inch along the channels of a darkened way,
Screeching all pain and knowledge from the pure
Simplicity of brain to the level of this twisted game we play.

BOOK SEVEN

THE STEPS OF BAST

UGLINESS must ever have been of woman:
 Woman would rather have been the simpler act.
"I am far too logical to fulfill my function!" men cried,
And lifting their heads, shouted with a logical delight toward
   the sun.

The calm to dissociate fragments of life was here;
The unclean was not admitted and there was light—
So many hairs plucked from the shining universal beard.
All declared the womb a seditious fertility.

Oh, great and mighty thought! Oh, pillar of fire!
Every female is the reincarnation of some cat upon the steps of
   Bast.
Therefore rejoice with the plaintive reeds along the liquid Nile,
Be glad that your sides have other shapes and that your laughter
   breaks.

From the fearful weight of stone, ape-eyes turn in their rim.
This is a world directly gutted by numbed birth and death,
Timeless instinct and the fluctuant flame of curiosity.
Life sprang and crept and agonized, from rock and sea, and
   vast black loam.

"I am the root, the excrement and flowering; my hands are the
   interplay of meaning;
I am dancing upon two earth-curved legs about the fire;
I am the animal savage God, drinking my first dark bitter
   wine;
The sleep is my sleep, the waking my waking, the taming my
   taming."

The corn is swaying in rich far acres and there is no other gold;
The slow oxen have the brazen sounds of low flutes and trum-
    peting;
There are men who sit in the villages with their brains the grist
    of words:
And all this is the growth in the several heads of men.

Come, shoulder your way out of your varied skin,
Out of your vicious sex-urge and masked prancing;
Shoulder the burden of cities, of thought and of wings:
Have no more of your stamping, but demand clean circum-
    cision.

Lift your heads to the brink and let them spin.
You who turn always to the sun, the round hung sun,
Leave the moon and its evil ways to women and the night—
Cats that stir on the step and howl their pulsing life-watch.

Every tower and every turret undermined by the craft
Of secret invert gods and image-worshiping,
Shuddering back against the too loud shout of the evil-exor-
    cisers:
Hard men, in wide gold surplices, airing their warrior chants.

"Yet our hearts would beat with an age-old drum,
And the women would hear and come to us from their idols
    and out of their temples,"
Spoke the blunt-mouthed men, with the sudden logic of beasts,
And rising, strode away from their freedom, thrusting behind
    them the structure of their cities.

AND AS I CAME OUT FROM THE TEMPLES

AND as I came out from the temples and stared,
  I saw to the left and to the right the fair-haired,
The sea-eyed, the rough-throated and the slender young.
Out of the temples I take breath, and count among
The hoard, all the resilient sheen of armor and of sword.

My people, O my people! Lift the sea of your eyes
So that I may remember life from the incensed halls.
Let me drown in the reflection of your corn-gold life;
Spare me and lift my soul with the shoot of many glances.

Behind the temple, the sun has set and risen to the gazing ones.
The smell of incense has given way to salt tang as the high seas
    run,
Boats drawn high to each strand and companion shore.
My sons are waving from four hills, like four
Sovereign eagles, with memories that the father has forgotten.

My children, O my children! How you do sway, my children!
For each newborn I feared and hated and wept against the
    wall;
I died, my face and tears within my hands; the palms wore thin
    and wet,
Wept until at last I learnt to feel one with old trees and new
    shoots.

My land! Land where my children and my people wait!

After man's passion for strange lands grew tired within me,
I went to the well that still holds fruit beside the desert sea.

JEW AMONGST RUINS

JEW with the Syrian arch
 Suspended about your shoulders,
Cerulean sky quiet in an oriental noon,
The long black shroud of immutable silence
Has drawn to the bone of you.
Your face is the closed door to cities,
And in the immobile length of figure,
The sphinx mounts in changing shifts of sand.

What is time to the yellow grains
That stir in momentary plains within your soul?

Messiah pauses when the last ache of your loins
Has spent itself between the bowl and bed,
Renouncing the easy thought
Toward some sad-songed constellation.

All things are to be sung
In the high sweet head tones of a desert pipe.

Walls were only made for weeping,
That and the walls of flesh,
Wailing to the omnipresence of Messiah.

Oh, the exquisite curse of loneliness!
What has the more desert flute of tranquillity
Than this shrill plucking
Up to the cerulean blue of an oriental noon?

Pull back to the shadow, Jew.
The gates of Syria have crumbled out of age.
You live and stand in the tomorrow,
And your wings are the eagle's,
Bearing many suns.

THE CAVES ARE SAD WHERE
THE ARCHAEOLOGISTS STOOD

THE caves are sad where the archaeologists stood.
 Out of the old brow of the rock, the wrinkles deepen.
The trees whisper like grave ancestors and draw the occult
    hood
Over the horizon, over the head, over the unspoken men.

In museums, small bones show their tender stone.
The Neanderthal ponderously thinks his fossiled dream.
And Egypt in his case admits more weary bone,
Draws the great dust from its sleep and tends the sleeper's
    scheme.

Over in Wales are rivers more timeless than the fish.
The Black Kelt still chews leathery bark,
Motioning the wiry runt to pass the sour dish.
Off on the high cracked crag, the first pipe peals the dark.

Out of the freak chastened valleys in the night,
Where the tired life dodges, each from his several pride,
Up to the glistening hole where the worm sucks out of sight,
And the weak-eyed fish must hide.

The scavenger dog, a retribute for past,
Suffers the moon to drop with little more than a whine.
And the woman, pulling her hair, bursts from the weight at
    last,
And the man stares stark as the pine, the untouched pine.

The dreadful feet of the hills come to an infant's cry,
Animal step of the wolf, and the hawk, and the fox,
Bearing apart the soul, trampling moon, quiet sky,
Burnt to the earliest god, deep in the caverned rocks.

The rustle of textbooks, over the shallow dish
Of the river, more timeless than the powerless pad of leather
    and the anemic archaeologist,
Shouting the source of the river, more timeless than the fish,
Collecting bone from the marrow of the past and breath of the
    fluctuant mist.

PENELOPE

SOFTLY the waves lip along the line.
    Tired trees, a little dreaming.
Dusk. Two pointed fingers up.

"Penelope!"
        The listless-fingered Odysseus
        Mouthed at the warm ripe figs
        That bent the twigs.

"Penelope, why does your hair
In one wide wood hang down
From Ithacan cliffs?
I had thought it love,
A tearful habit, watering the sea.
Now I see a fluctuant star
Translated in your mind
Into the bitter-sweet word
Of transcending loneliness.
In barren lights the colonnades reflect . . .
The flat pink steps
Where dogs once licked lascivious wounds,
And in the drunken air
The drunken lovers spewed;

(Translucent star, a transient bed,
Jagged stone and shrill Ithacan pipe,
Vast space, immutable sea.
Out of the head, Athens, from out the head,
The black ship, the wine-red sea,
The tear, the sigh, the irrevocable dead,
What still hand here and head between the knees.)

133

Where too you wove with transient thread
A dreary pattern of eternal siege;
A black ship battered
And sad bones bleached out
With soft whales' sperm
And silvered round with rime.
Pale tears became the threads
To that shroud nuptial gown.

Hear now from jagged hills
Through cypress trees
The shrill glad pipes of Ithaca
And see here once again
Who lies against your feet,
Tangling the beaded honey of his locks,
Penelope!"

      The listless-fingered Odysseus
      Mouthed, smiling, at the warm ripe figs
      That bent a burden to the twigs.

ORPHEUS. THREE ECLOGUES

I

ORPHEUS. CALLIOPE. THE BEASTS.

ORPHEUS:
 I DIED, my face and tears within my hands;
  The palms wore thin with wet,
 Remarked the tideless sea of swaying lands,
 And plucked and fluted and could not forget.

CALLIOPE:
 Young son of Thrace, out-staring stars,
 Binding your song to death and sleep,
 Rise and inveigle Hades and entangle Mars,
 And tug from death your strands of harvest wheat.

ORPHEUS:
 Old woman, Mother, coming from clean day
 Into my unclear and peculiar pain,
 O sit as I do, ranting on this clay,
 Drown in these tears, drown in my perpendicular rain.

CALLIOPE:
 What is this lyre? What your unriddled action?
 O why this running of distracted sense?
 Several objects speak your sorrow and dissatisfaction;
 The repercussions of this dying are immense.

ORPHEUS:
 These arms, Mother, O these arms are empty.
 The earth is round; the trees and slopes
 Unquestionably full, while I freeze into sterility.
 You know the bottom of seas, wells, and streams,
 Where will the songs go now and where the hopes?

Must I delight the twisted root and sea gull's vacant
    screams?
When I stood naked by my wedding bed, Eurydice,
While the snake dipped away its dreadful eye,
I who had danced with innocents so prettily
Drew then from Acheron the wind of Charon's sigh.

CALLIOPE:

The virginities of ghosts stand in uncharted quiet;
Speak about beaches and the waves will find their end,
Run back upon impeccable feet into the hollows, let
Mist sink your words where shades will apprehend.

THE BEASTS:

We prance along the wind,
We whimper tentatively:
Be careful of dead places.
Be careful of dead places.
Who are wiser than we
That eye the day with primal panic,
Draw near from crags and caverns,
From forests and furred corners?
We therefore whisper tentatively:
Be careful of dead places.

ORPHEUS:

What are those tongues that stutter instead of being dead?
Where do I stand alone? In what moment have I not de-
    served the past?
Let me string my lyre with some senescent thread,
To twang the one grave note and breathe at last.

THE BEASTS:

We are growing dull with the sound of Orpheus,
He who once sang so prettily through the woman, Eu-
    rydice;

136

We are so nearly sleeping, so close to our beginning.
The little child, the tired enchanter,
Must enter the steaming womb;
The son of Calliope must go down to Hades.

II

ORPHEUS. CHARON. THE SHADES.

ORPHEUS:

Old Man who punt the Acheron, what is Hades like?
For Night and Day converge so in my mind,
The one's decay and weed and spawn of all that men dis-
    like,
The other's light and flourish, strong and somewhat kind,
I am unable to think of direct end or direct beginning:
The weird kernel of the I stands sexless and devoid,
Mere energy that lives from self, unloved, unsinning,
The end of all that living once enjoyed.

CHARON:

In sleep we disarrange the day,
Awake we try to give arrangement to that sleep.
There is the Greek who used to play
Upon the ideal image in some upper deep,
There are the miscellaneous thoughts from all the shades
    I bear.
Each object has its ego-center and its strength,
Its ageless light and microcosmic fear:
A nautilus may die yet through the length
Of time and inordinate generation impress a self, basic and
    endurable;
The fact cannot be outfaced of being and not being,
Of moving and not moving; that which we know remains
    forever knowable.
The strong are a flavor and a textural feeling;
Theirs is the bravery of the titillating and obscure

To hold themselves abruptly in high air and spin:
The purity of wind and straining sail are unalterably pure,
And each, completing its own function in
The span of a man or the inevitable eon,
Finally and roundly sings the Whole in its all-designing
    conscience:
One man awake, the others still below; one man to stir and
    yawn,
To stamp the calm and turbulence of World with delicate
    defiance.

ORPHEUS:

    Father of this dulled river without source or sea,
    Lean mad bat, dangling upon the sharp point of your pole,
    I have swept beasts away from death till they would die for
        me;
    I could not keep compact the slopes of Eurydice and the
        tender factions of her soul.

THE SHADES:

    When you have reached your destination,
    Found the sharp even avenues, the sound of leaves,
    Noises infinitely quieter than pacing insects,
    When you have touched upon the end and destiny of grief,
    Along those paths neither shining, subtle, void or tranquil,
    You must lean through all your warmed perceptions to
        grasp that shade:
    You will know that it possess hands though you see no
        hand;
    You will know that it is as a woman should be, walking
        and not weak.
    Turn abruptly. Do not look about. Do not stare from side
        to side.
    We are lonely for your singing, Orpheus. Take back the
        woman Eurydice.

ORPHEUS:

Eurydice! Eurydice! Out of the Grave!
This is the smoothed beard of Olympus.

CHARON:

Punt, punt over the soundless water,
Sigh, sigh, die in the tideless stream.
Tears of vindictive virgins,
The negators and castrated of the cities of sleep.
Weep, weep over the dull green liquid.
As you drown I gather you up
Who may never murmur along the bank
Or pluck the crisp blunt reeds.
Punt, punt over the soundless water,
Sigh, sigh, die in the tideless stream.

III

ORPHEUS.   CHARON.   THE SHADES.   EURYDICE.

ORPHEUS:

Each corpse stretched wide its dry distending hands
And each skull dreamed an elongating song,
And every heart, an hourglass of filtered sands,
Heard every grain proclaim the right from wrong.

EURYDICE:

I am rocking the world with the ripple of my thighs,
Drenched in ridiculous laughter;
Over the river of woe, away from the valley of exacting
    sighs,
Striding toward the upper globe, I follow after.

ORPHEUS:

First I became a note from my own breath,
Stopping all sounds but those that rose too high or low;

Entering the vacant hall I plucked the mute command of
 death,
And all my intuitions were alert to perceive and know.
Pluto cloaked, and glared with lidless eyes,
And every evil mocked and swiveled and returned,
Lifting great sides to feed their virulent sighs,
While through the whole concept of death the leprous
 sperm whales churned.
I, with all my senses straining by,
Ran chanting on to recreate the intolerant vision
That leaped to hound me back with rant and embryo cry
Into a frightful innocence of spawn and automat precision;
The ugliest mouth cracked, and I filled its emptiness;
Briefly I strummed my lyre, and the tired hag sprang
 luminous,
The mass-head of infinity turned with repercussive weari-
 ness,
And I heard from the nonexistent dome a murmured,
 Orpheus!

EURYDICE:
A few steps now and the past and the immediate will be
 mine;
I will lean myself to the wind and nibble the sensation,
Passionately grasp the oval bowls of wine,
Taste and tamper, have precise delight in the minutest tilt
 of inclination.

ORPHEUS:
Yet my entering that world is not their dying:
Eurydice, I am fearful of the dead and the unborn.
When you died, I died with you; the rocks and birds and
 beasts came to me whimpering,
And even the Gods upon Olympus were pedantic and for-
 lorn.

A little of my soul grew tired and winged:
How do I know that I am not nursed under the usual
     bough—asleep?
Old Charon wisely surmised: "Know what is fact and
     what is dreamed."
So much of my searching has been a sensual passage
     through the deep.

EURYDICE:
Orpheus, I shall tell you that I am. I shape! I shape!
Here is the well-placed head, the delicate trace of vein;
Through wrists and breasts whence these tattered drapes
     escape,
I put my hand upon my heart and feel its action once again.

ORPHEUS:
Be careful of dead places. Be careful of dead places.
They burst on me and stood in painful circles.
Why should I receive more from the dead than from the
     simple graces?
In Hades the very warmth of tears drew taut and dropped
     thin icicles.

EURYDICE:
I am whole. I was dead. It is harvest in delicious Thrace.
Argos has drooped and prompted one kind eye alone to
     stare;
Into my lungs I draw the whole full breathing of a race
Whose mother hand is my delight, whose cries are my
     despair.

ORPHEUS:
I am turning, Eurydice, turning . . .
It is the wonder of a sleeping child that turns upon its
     sleep:

141

A doubt without discerning,
A shy hand stretched along the edgeless wall where fearful
    shadows weep.

EURYDICE:
    In my palms lie these two clear efforts of my eyes,
    The very essence of this tormented moment.

THE SHADES:
    O son of Calliope, do not turn upon yourself:
    Every hour a new doubt assails the grave.
    If you do not turn back, the past will live with you again
    And you will be the immediate parent;
    Your song will weave each glinting object with its shade.
    Even now you slant your eyes and swerve;
    Old Charon's listless tune completely fills our ears.

EURYDICE:
    Orpheus, be quick. Be brief. I will bear you a child among
        the dead.
    There is no doubt or crying, mind or fact.
    Stretch in the reeds beside the Acheron before all hope has
        sped
    With formal hope, far from the intent action and the act.

THE SHADES:
    Birds and beasts, rocks and fish of the sea,
    Watch how the lidless pools absorb to themselves
    The improbable adventure without a ripple.
    Orpheus, springing towards the wonder of the dead un-
        dead,
    Clasped to himself the concave image and the negative,
    Drew to his fluting breath the strange distortion
    And kissed and kissed again all that contracted in,

That which had sighed wind-wise and rushed back upon
    its end,
Clutching the tideless water, tiring the river reeds,
A chanting tearful lover, impassioned and complaining.
Birds and beasts, rocks and fish of the sea,
Allow us to return to you your living:
Though Hades is kind to those who remember and reclaim
    sleep,
Leave what may be the absolute of death to us, the proper
    dead.

The Yale Series of Younger Poets is designed to afford a publishing medium for the work of young men and women who have not yet secured wide public recognition. It will include only verse which seems to give good promise for the future of American poetry—to the development of which it is hoped that the Series may prove a stimulus. Communications concerning manuscripts should be addressed to the Editor of The Yale Series of Younger Poets, in care of the Yale University Press, New Haven, Connecticut.